DEC 5 -	DATE DUE	
DEC 1 4		
APR 2 0 2000		
NOV 2 5 2000		
DEC 2 1 2000		
NOV 2 0 2001		
MAY 1 - 2002		
MAR 2 4 '03		

Evening Gray, Morning Red

Evening Gray, Morning Red

A Ready-to-Read Handbook of American Weather Wisdom

BARBARA WOLFF

Macmillan Publishing Co., Inc.
NEW YORK
Collier Macmillan Publishers
LONDON

To Ben and Rudi

Macmillan Publishing Co., Inc.
866 Third Avenue, New York, N.Y. 10022
Collier Macmillan Canada, Ltd.
Printed in the United States of America

10 9 8 7 6 5 4 3 2 1

LIBRARY OF CONGRESS CATALOGING IN PUBLICATION DATA
Wolff, Barbara.   Evening gray, morning red.   (Ready-to-read handbook)
    SUMMARY: A handbook of weather forecasting based on rhymes, sayings,
and signs used in America for centuries. Includes instructions for building a
simple weather vane. 1. Weather lore—United States—Juvenile literature.
[1. Weather lore] I. Title.
QC998.W64 1976   551.6′31   76—15640   ISBN 0—02—793320—2

Contents

Introduction   7

Clouds   11

Sky Color   21

Sun and Moon   25

Birds, Insects and Animals   29

Plants   35

Wind   41

Other Weather Signs   51

How to Make a Wind Vane   58

Introduction

Long ago, people depended on
signs in nature to tell the weather.
There were no weather reports
in newspapers.
There was no TV or radio
to give weather programs.
Farmers watched the sky before
a storm. Travelers watched
the leaves blowing in the wind.
Sailors watched the clouds changing.
After a while, people began making up
rhymes about the weather.
The rhymes helped them to remember
the weather signs.

These rhymes were so popular that before long, printers put them into books called almanacs.

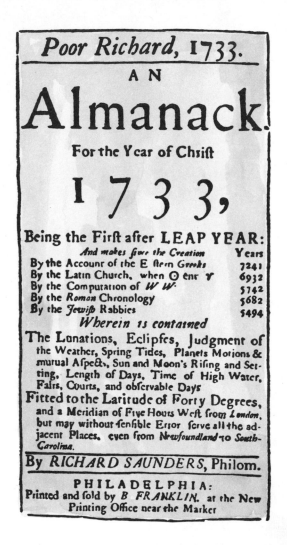

The almanacs also contained
interesting and useful facts about
the stars, the calendar, cooking,
planting, traveling, and keeping well.
The first American almanacs to have
weather sayings were printed before 1700.
Since New England was settled very early,
much weather lore comes from there.
Many of these weather rhymes
are still used today.
They can help you look for the same
weather signs people studied long ago.

Clouds

The clouds are getting bigger.
They look like mountains.
Ben wants to get home
before the rain starts.

Can you guess the weather
by looking at the clouds?
There are many kinds of clouds.
Some clouds are fat and fluffy.
Others are thin and wispy.
They can be high in the sky or low.

When clouds look like rocks and towers,
The earth will have many showers.

cumulus

The higher the clouds,
The better the weather.

When wooly clouds come this way,
No rain will spoil the day.

"Wooly clouds" look like
little white puffs.

alto - cumulus

Wooly sheep in the sky
Will bring raindrops by and by.

The white puffs have grown bigger.
They look like a flock of sheep.
The sheep are crowded together.
That means rain or snow may come soon.

Strato- cumulus

Mackerel sky, mackerel sky,
Not long wet, not long dry.

These clouds look like fish scales.
The weather will change soon.

A sunny shower
Won't last half an hour.

Is the sun shining through
the rain clouds?
The sky will soon be blue.

CLOUD CHART

Good Weather Clouds

Some good weather clouds
look like wisps of hair.
Others look like feathers in the sky.

Or like wooly puffs.

Storm Clouds

When the wooly clouds begin
to look like this, it means
the weather will change.

These storm clouds
are called thunderheads.
They are very tall and
have flat tops.

Clouds that look like webs
are still another sign that rain is coming.

Sky Color

Ben and John are watching the sunset.
"I bet it will rain tomorrow," John says.
John does not want it to rain.
He wants a nice day because
he and Ben are going to the beach.

The color of the sky can tell us
if rain is on the way.
A gray sky does not always
mean a storm is coming.
But a red sunrise may mean a day of rain.

Evening red and morning gray
Send the traveler on his way.

A clear red evening sky means
there are no clouds coming toward us.
If a gray morning follows,
it may just be fog.
Morning fog usually clears quickly.

Evening gray and morning red
Send the traveler wet to bed.

Clouds in the sky at sunset make
the sky look gray. These clouds
are moving toward us.
The sunrise is still red and clear
because the clouds are not yet overhead.
When they reach us, it may rain.

Sun and Moon

Ben watches the moon from his bed.

It has a white ring around it.

Ben wonders why.

Have you ever seen a red moon,

or the sun with a ring around it?

The moon and sun can help tell you what

the weather will be like the next day.

When the sun or moon
Is in its house,
It will rain soon.

"House" means a ring or halo
around the moon.
A thin layer of clouds causes the ring.
When the clouds become thicker
and hide the sun or moon,
rain is very near.

Pale moon will rain,
Red moon will blow,
White moon will neither
Rain nor blow.

The moon looks pale and fuzzy
when a layer of clouds covers it.
The moon is red because there is
dust or smoke in the air. The moon
is white when the weather is clear.

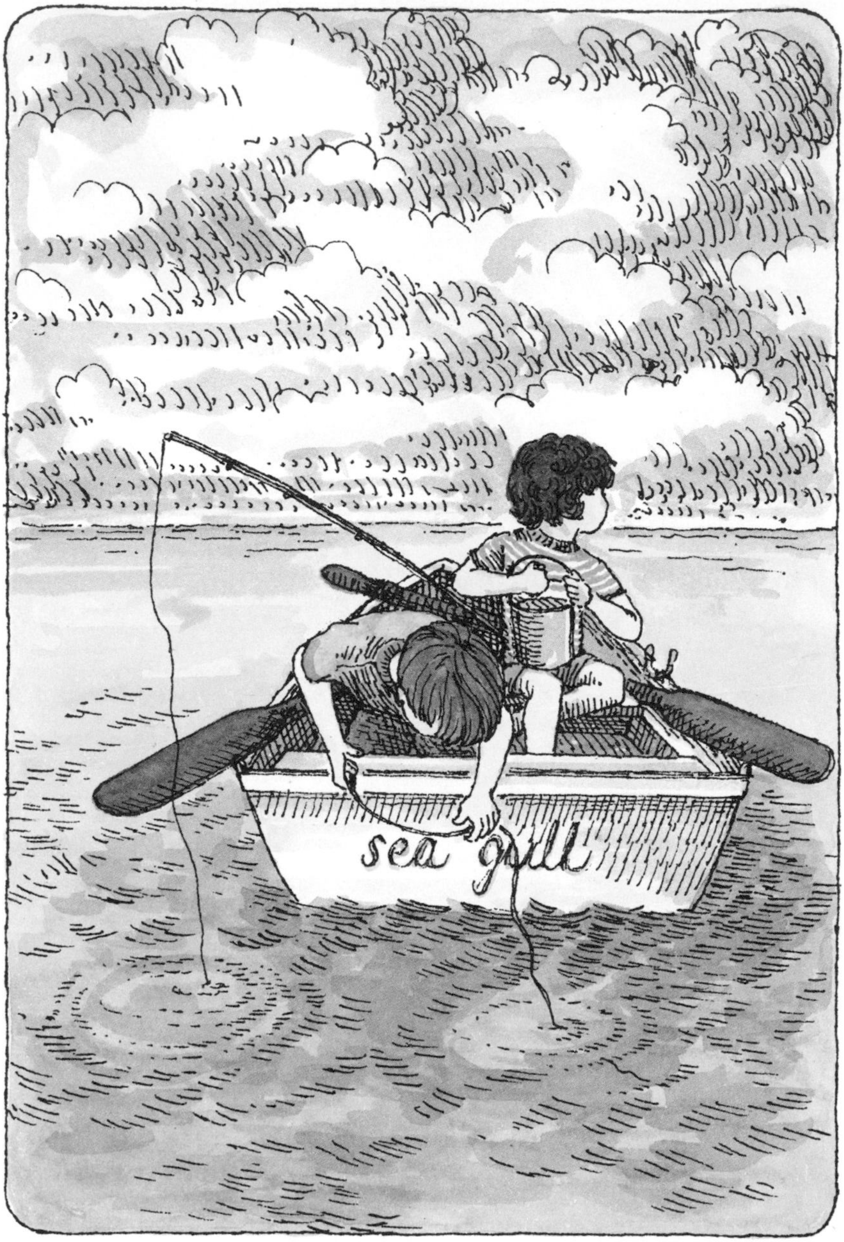
sea gull

Birds, Insects, and Animals

Ben is catching lots of fish.
"Where are the sea gulls today?
Are they all on the beach?"

Birds and animals may sense
when the weather is changing.
They show it in different ways.

Sea gull, sea gull,
Sitting on the sand;
It's never good weather
When you're on land.

Birds settle on the ground or in trees
when bad weather is coming.
Some people say it is because
the winds are stronger before a rain.
And wind makes it harder to fly.

Near the surface, quick to bite,
Catch your fish when rain's in sight.

Fishermen say that fish bite more
often when rain is on the way.
But nobody knows why.

Crickets and katydids
are good thermometers.
They chirp fast when it is warm.
Katydids chirp less and less
as it gets colder.

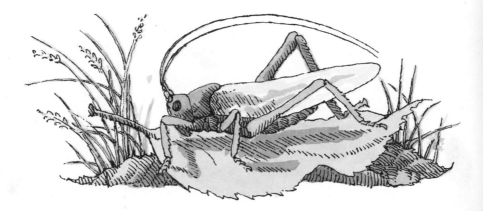

"Kate-ee-did-n't"	85°
"Kate-ee-did"	75°
"Kate-ee"	65°
"Kate"	55°

No more chirping. Fall is here.
Winter is coming.

A cow with its tail to the west
Makes weather the best.
A cow with its tail to the east
Makes weather the least.

This is a New England weather rhyme.
In most of the United States,
the west wind is a good weather wind.
The east wind is a rain wind.
Cows always stand with
their tails to the wind.
This makes a cow a good wind vane.

Plants

One morning, Ben goes out.

The grass is wet.

"Did it rain last night?

Will it rain today?

If it rains, it will spoil

our game," he thinks.

The streets are dry. The air is clear.

The moisture on the grass must be dew.

Dew is a sign of fair weather.

Plants can tell you other things

about the weather, too.

When the leaves
Show their backs,
It will rain.

A storm wind blows the leaves
over to show their backs.
The backs of most leaves
are lighter in color than the tops.
That is why the leaves seem to turn
light green in a storm wind.

When the laurel shuts its door,

That's when winter storms will roar.

Laurel leaves close up with the cold.

The more tightly they close,

the colder it is.

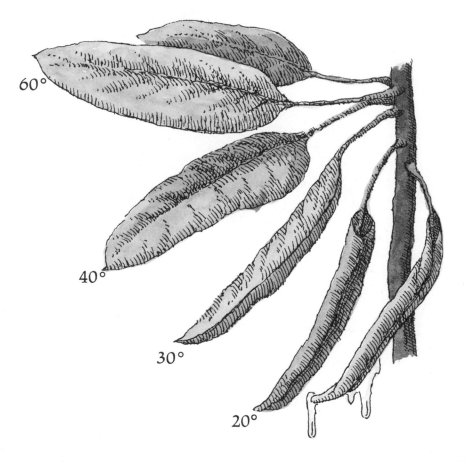

When the dew is on the grass,
Rain will never come to pass.

Dew forms on the grass
when the air above is cool and dry
and the air near the ground
is warm and damp.

Moss dry, sunny sky.

Moss wet, rain we'll get.

Moss is like a sponge.

It soaks up water from the air.

When moss feels very wet, it may rain.

Wind

The wind is bending the trees.

The sky is gray.

"I wish it would snow," Ben thinks.

"I want to use my new sled."

Wind and sky could have told Ben

that snow is on the way.

The north wind does blow,
And we will have snow.

The north wind comes from the
icy north and brings cold weather.
If there is a lot of moisture in the air
as well, it will bring snow.

When the wind is from the east,
It's not good for man or beast.

This is another New England
rhyme. It, too, tells us that
an east wind usually brings rain.
In winter, wind from the northeast
often means heavy snow.

When the forest whispers
And the mountain roars,
Then close the windows
And shut the doors.

A storm is coming!
Winds start to blow
high above the earth.
They reach the mountaintops first.
They roar through the trees.
And even if the winds are still
only a whisper in the valley,
it is a sign that a storm is coming.

June, too soon;

July, stand by;

August, look out!

September, you will remember;

October, all over.

Hurricanes are dangerous seasonal
storms. They have very strong winds.
This rhyme tells you which are
the hurricane months.
But they are not "all over"
till the end of October.

WIND CHART

How hard is the wind blowing?

Is it just a strong breeze, or is it a gale?

Is it a storm wind or a hurricane?

In 1806, Admiral Beaufort made up

a wind chart for his sailors.

The Beaufort Scale of Wind Force

is still used all over the world.

A chart also was made for use on land.

Here are some of the land signs.

Miles per hour

0-1	Calm
4-7	Light breeze
8-12	Gentle breeze
19-24	Fresh breeze
25-31	Strong breeze
32-38	Gale
47-54	Strong gale
64-72	Storm
above 73	Hurricane

Smoke goes straight up.

Leaves rustle and
a wind vane moves.

Leaves and twigs move.
A light flag flutters.

Small trees begin to sway.

Large branches move.
Umbrellas turn inside out.

Whole trees sway.
It is hard to walk
against the wind.

Branches break from trees.

Houses are damaged.

The countryside is badly damaged.
Sometimes people are killed.

Other Weather Signs

"It's fun toasting marshmallows tonight!
The smoke isn't getting
into our eyes," Ben said.

Smoke can tell us about the weather, too.
And so can rainbows, and stars,
and the sounds of things around us.

When smoke descends,
Good weather ends.

A rain wind will often
make smoke drift downward.

Rainbow in the morning,
Sailor take warning.
Rainbow toward night,
Sailor's delight.

A rainbow in the morning
may mean a storm is on the way.
A rainbow in the evening shows
that the storm has passed.

When the stars begin to hide,
Rain will make you go inside.

Thin clouds over the stars
make them look dim.
The dimmer the stars,
the closer the rain.

The farther the sight,
The nearer the rain.

When distant things are seen very clearly,
it may be a sign that rain is coming.
That is because the strong winds that come
before a storm blow away any haze in the air.

Sounds traveling far and wide,
A stormy day will betide.

Farmers used to say that they
could hear bad weather coming.
They meant that faraway sounds seemed
to echo when a storm was on its way.

Rain before seven,
Clear before eleven.

Morning showers often end quickly.
But not always!

How to Make
a Wind Vane

Changes in the wind often mean

that the weather will change.

A wind vane always points

to where the wind is coming from.

Farmers and sailors have been using

wind vanes since anyone can remember.

Weather forecasters still use them today.

You can make your own wind vane.

What you will need:

Aluminum foil pan

Long nail with a head

2 washers

Plasteline
clay

Scrap wood
about 14 inches long,
1/4 to 1/2 inch thick

Scrap wood
about 14 inches long,
at least 3/4 inch thick.
You can also use a dowel.

Heavy piece of wood
about 8 inches square,
at least 3/4 inch thick

Waterproof glue, hammer, ruler, scissors, crayons

With a crayon write
NORTH, EAST, SOUTH, WEST
on the square piece of wood.
Use the picture as a guide.

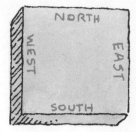

Use a crayon and ruler
to make a big X on the wood.
Draw the lines from
corner to corner.

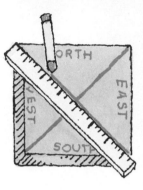

Draw a circle
where the lines cross.

Put plenty of glue
in the circle.

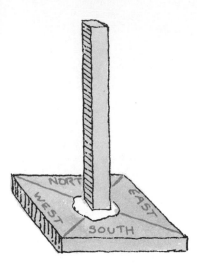

Stand one end of the thick
stick on the spot of glue.
Press it there until it
begins to hold.
Then let it dry
for a few hours.

Put a mark in the middle
of the thin stick.

Place it on some scrap wood
or on the ground outside.
Hammer the nail into the mark
to make a hole.

Wiggle the nail around
and pull it out.

With a crayon draw
a big triangle and a little one
on the bottom of the foil pan.

Cut out the triangles.
Glue the triangles
to the ends
of the thin stick.
It should look like this.

Put a washer on the nail.

Put the point of the nail
through the hole in the stick.

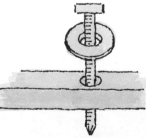

Put the other washer
on the nail.
Hammer the nail
into the top
of the post.

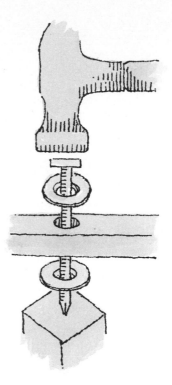

If the arrow
does not turn easily,
loosen the nail.

Stick small bits of clay
to the front of the arrow
until it balances.
Make sure it still turns easily.

Now the wind vane is ready to use.

Pick a flat spot outdoors.
Face the direction where
the sun sets at night.
Set the wind vane on the ground so that
the word WEST points in that direction.

Watch the wind turn the arrow.
The point of the arrow will show you
where the wind is coming from.